KINGFISHER
READERS

level

W9-BGB-704

Seasons

Thea Feldman

KINGFISHER
NEW YORK

KINGFISHER
LONDON & NEW YORK

Distributed in the U.S. and Canada by Macmillan,
175 Fifth Ave., New York, NY 10010

Library of Congress Cataloging-in-Publication data
has been applied for.

Series editor: Thea Feldman
Literacy consultant: Ellie Costa, Bank Street School for Children, New York

ISBN: 978-0-7534-6897-5 (HB)
ISBN: 978-0-7534-6898-2 (PB)

Kingfisher books are available for special promotions
and premiums. For details contact: Special Markets
Department, Macmillan, 175 Fifth Ave.,
New York, NY 10010.

For more information, please visit
www.kingfisherbooks.com

Printed in China
9 8 7 6 5 4 3 2 1
1TR/0712/WKT/UG/105MA

Picture credits
The Publisher would like to thank the following for permission to reproduce their material.
Every care has been taken to trace copyright holders. However, if there have been unintentional
omissions or failure to trace copyright holders, we apologize and will, if informed, endeavor to make
corrections in any future edition.
Top = t; Bottom = b; Center = c; Left = l; Right = r
Cover Shutterstock/cappi thompson; Pages 3 Getty/AFP; 4–5 Shutterstock/Kotenko Oleksandr;
6 Shutterstock/Liudmila Evdochimova; 7 Shutterstock/jordache; 8–9 Photolibrary/Imagebroker;
10–11 Photolibrary/Peter Arnold Images; 12 Photolibrary/Animals Animals; 13 Shutterstock/Mayovskyy
Andrew; 14 Shutterstock/Dmitry Naumov; 15 Photolibrary/DK Stock; 16 inset Shutterstock/Elena Elisseeva;
16 Shutterstock/WDG Photo; 17 Shutterstock/Irrinn0215; 18 Shutterstock/Margaret M. Stewart;
19 Shutterstock/Vishnevskiy Vasily; 20–21 Alamy/Corbis Bridge; 22 Shutterstock/Sonya Etchison;
23 Photolibrary/Erik Isakson/Tetra; 24 Shutterstock/Lawrence Cruciana; 25 Shutterstock/nikkytok;
26–27 Alamy/Chad Ehlers; 28 Shutterstock/Subbotina Anna; 29t Corbis/Andrew Parkinson;
29b Shutterstock/Marty Ellis; 30c Photolibrary/Jose Luis Pelaez/Iconica; 30b Corbis/Ted Horowitz;
31c Shutterstock/Brocreative; 31b Corbis/ Dann Tardiff/ Blend

It is snowing!

What **season** is it?

It is **winter**!

It is cold in winter.

Snow can fall from the clouds.

Do you like snow?

When you go outside in winter you wear a warm coat.

You put on mittens and a hat.

You wear boots.

And you need a scarf too!

Outside, many trees are bare.

They have lost their leaves.

Many plants do not grow flowers in winter.

The sun sets early in the
evening too.

Some animals find warm places
to sleep in winter.

These bears are sleeping
in a cave.

The animals will sleep
until winter is over.

Winter lasts three months.

What season comes
after winter?

Spring!

It gets warm in spring.

Sometimes it rains.

The sun shines a lot.

The days get longer.

In spring, new leaves
grow on trees.

New flowers grow on plants.

Animals wake up from their winter sleep.

Many animals have babies
in spring.

Spring lasts for three months.

What comes after spring?

Summer!

It is hot in summer.

The sun is strong.

The days are long.

There is more time to
play outside!

There is no school in summer.

What do you like to do instead?

You can have a picnic.

You can go swimming.

There are many fun things
to do!

Trees have green leaves
in summer.

Plants have colorful flowers.

Animals have a lot to eat.

Summer lasts for three months.

What season comes
after summer?

Fall!

It is cool in fall.

The wind blows more.

The days get shorter.

The sun sets earlier.

Leaves turn red,
yellow, and brown.

Many plants stop
growing flowers.

Some birds fly away.

Some animals gather food
for when fall is over.

Fall lasts for three months.

What season comes after fall?

Winter!

Many places have four seasons.
Some places have fewer.

winter

spring

The seasons come one after another, year after year.

Which season do you like best?

summer

fall

Glossary

fall the season that comes after summer, when the weather gets cooler

season a time that can be several months long, when the same kind of weather happens every year

snow frozen water that falls from clouds as snowflakes

spring the season that comes after winter, when the weather starts to get warmer

summer the warmest season of the year

winter the coldest season of the year